C000227697

BEETLE*Mania*

BEETLE*Mania*

Paul Wager

Grange
BOOKS

Published by Grange Books
An Imprint of Grange Books PLC
The Grange
Grange Yard
London SE1 3AG

This edition published 1995

ISBN 1 85627 644 9

Produced by
Bison Books Ltd
Kimbolton House
117A Fulham Road
London SW3 6RL

Printed in Spain

PAGE ONE: The fearsome
back end of a classic Baja
Bug.

PAGES TWO-THREE: Raised
chassis, wide tires and a
driving experience light
years away from that of
the basic Beetle.

RIGHT: A license plate that
speaks for itself.

Contents

The People's Car

Such is the enduring appeal and ingenious simplicity of the Volkswagen Beetle that the vehicle which was originally designed to provide low-cost working-class mobility in prewar Germany can be found, 50 years later, all over the world and decorated in colors and driven at speeds undreamt of by the car's designers.

At the time of writing, the Beetle has passed its 50th birthday, and is still being produced in factories in both Mexico and Brazil; production ceased for a while in Brazil, but was restarted recently when the government identified the need for an affordable small car and provided tax breaks for the company. Over 21 million Beetles have been manufactured since production started, and since 1972, when it overtook the Ford Model T, the Beetle has been the most-produced single car model in history – it has even been voted the Car of the Century.

The world's most popular car, which is so full of character that most owners endow them with nicknames, was born in the dark days of Nazi Germany, as part of Hitler's dream to produce a car for the masses – a Volkswagen, or "People's Car" – which the average German family could afford.

The designer of the Beetle was Ferdinand Porsche, who had designed his first car at the age of 21 and who had worked for most of the great names in prewar German automotive manufacturing such as Lohner, Austro-Daimler, Mercedes, Daimler-Benz and Steyr, before opening his own design bureau in 1930. At least ten years earlier Porsche had designed a small, affordable car for Daimler, but the project halted at the prototype stage. In 1931 he set his staff to designing a vehicle which featured a lightweight three-

PREVIOUS PAGES: A 1977 Beetle with a modified V8 engine.

ABOVE: 1962 was the last year for the full-length folding fabric sunroof. It was replaced by a steel sliding version for 1963.

LEFT: Flawless graphics are a major part of the drag racing scene.

RIGHT: The tiny rear lamp assembly with top-mounted brake lights was changed for 1955 to improve safety.

OPPOSITE PAGE: A personalized license plate is just one way of making your Beetle stand out from the other millions.

RIGHT: None of them standard, but no two the same – who said the Cal look cars all look identical?

BELOW: The classic Cal look – lowered, dechromed and running on those classy Empi 8-spoke replicas.

cylinder radial engine, with fully-independent suspension and was able to transport four adults in comfort at 100 kph (62 mph). The price was to be kept at a sufficiently low level to make it affordable to the masses.

Porsche tried to sell his idea to the German motor industry; initially the motorcycle manufacturer Zündapp, was interested, although the project was canceled largely due to the uncertain economic climate in Germany at the time, and was subsequently taken up by NSU, another motorcycle manufacturer wishing to expand. However, although three prototypes of the NSU car were constructed, the project was abandoned.

The NSU design bore many similarities to the Beetle. Problems with the rotary engines in the Zündapp prototype had resulted in the use of the four-cylinder, air-cooled horizontally-opposed engine we know today, and the space-saving torsion-bar suspension system, revolutionary in a car of this kind, had only recently been patented by Porsche's firm.

Although his small-car project had been crushed twice, Porsche was given fresh enthusiasm by Hitler's announcement at the 1933 Berlin Motor Show of his plans to produce a small car for the average family. Following a meeting between Hitler and Porsche, a contract was signed in 1934 for Porsche to construct three prototypes and deliver them for testing within ten months. Despite Porsche's experience in small-car design, constant changes were necessary to meet Hitler's target price of RM 990, and the prototypes were not delivered until October, 1936.

A wide range of different engines were tried in the prototypes, but the eventual choice was an air-cooled, horizontally-opposed, four-stroke, four-cylinder engine, developed by the Porsche engineer Franz Reimspiess. This was the engine which was to remain unchanged in its basic concept throughout the production life of the Beetle.

Despite numerous delays in the construction of the factory, public support continued unabated; the car was to be marketed by an unusual scheme, by which individuals could buy the cars at the rate of five Reichsmarks per week; once the payments had been made, the car would be delivered. With the outbreak of war, none of the buyers ever received the car, and it was not until a court case against Volkswagen was settled in 1961, that they were offered either DM100 compensation, or DM600 off the price of a new car.

The outbreak of war meant that Hitler canceled all projects which could not be completed by the end of 1939, and so production of the KdF-wagen ("Kraft durch Freude", or "Strength-through-joy" car) as Hitler called it, was suspended. The factory was eventually requisitioned by the Reich Air Ministry, and the factory management took on jobs such as manufacturing portable army stoves, in order to keep the plant afloat.

Some 630 standard sedans were produced during the war for government use, and the main output of the factory was military vehicles. In an attempt to keep his KdF project alive, Porsche had adapted the design to produce a Jeep-type vehicle, using a simple open body on the Beetle chassis, which used a limited-slip differential instead of four-wheel drive, and reduction gearing to raise ground clearance. The resulting vehicle, known as the "Kübelwagen," or "Bucket Car," was so successful, that Allied personnel often kept and used captured examples. Military versions of the standard sedan were also produced, including the Type 87, which used four-wheel drive and was fitted with a roller at the front, to help it clear large obstacles.

LEFT: An oval-window 1957 Beetle poses in front of Pasadena railway station.

ABOVE: Sherm Glas's 1966 1300 – owned from new and lovingly restored during the 1980s.

RIGHT: Many enthusiasts reckon the 1950s produced the finest Beetles.

Following the end of the Second World War, the factory fell under the British zone of occupation and was used for vehicle repair; a small number of Kübelwagens were also constructed, using spare bodyshells and other parts found within the debris of the factory. The town was named Wolfsburg in 1945, after Count Werner von Schulenberg of Wolfsburg, who had been forced to give up his land for the project.

By the end of 1945 58 new Volkswagens had been produced, despite the fact that large areas of the plant were still badly damaged. In 1946 the factory was ordered to produce 1000 cars per month in order to escape closure and in the end it just escaped, producing 10,020 cars during 1946. In 1947, the first exports of the Volkswagen were made, when the Dutch agent took five cars back with him to sell in Holland.

Although production had already increased, further expansion in output was necessary to make the plant viable, especially as the cars were difficult to sell abroad whilst the memories of Nazism lingered. However, in 1948 the fortunes of the plant suddenly changed, when the long-awaited German currency reform was announced. This resulted in a spending spree by a people unaccustomed to trusting paper money but fortunately, the slow sales had caused a stockpile to build up. Volkswagen received its

ABOVE: It may be California, but the license plate identifies this as a '67 Beetle, or *Käfer*, as the car is known in its homeland.

LEFT: A license plate that says it all . . .

RIGHT: Cool chrome and whitewalls are just as much at home on this '66 Bug as on a '57 T-Bird.

first foreign-currency income in this year, and in 1949, deliveries of completely-knocked-down [CKD] cars for construction in Ireland and Brazil began. Volkswagen desperately needed foreign currency, especially US dollars in order to purchase new plant equipment, so exports to the USA were vital.

Until 1953, Volkswagens were sold through an exclusive imported-car agency in New York, and the volume achieved was pitifully small; it was not until around 100 Volkswagen personnel were sent to the USA to form a proper export department, that sales began to grow, and by 1955 Volkswagen could be seen at the top of the imported-car sales charts, selling 28,097 cars in the

LEFT: Just 696 Hebmüller cabriolets were constructed – the company was bankrupted by fire in 1949.

BELOW: The high-riding Baja Bug style was born from Mexican desert racing.

RIGHT: Not many folk can claim to drive a '49 Volkswagen, especially the rare Hebmüller – only about 50 are thought to survive today in various stages of restoration.

year. Central to the car's success in the USA was the insistence on providing a comprehensive spares and service backup, with a fleet of factory-trained mechanics deployed around the country to educate the dealers on the unconventional Volkswagen.

In 1959, a new man took charge of the American operation: Carl Hahn. Later to become chairman of Volkswagen from 1982 until 1993, he made the decision to begin advertising the Volkswagen in America. After interviewing several agencies, he settled on Doyle Dayne Bernbach Inc., an agency well known for a unique creative style, and the advertisements forming this campaign have become classics over the years. Breaking with the traditional glamorous and fanciful style of automotive advertising prevalent at the time, the DDB advertisements pioneered an "honest" style, selling the cars on their virtues of dependability, quality and non-obsolescence. These campaigns made Volkswagen a household name: the 500,000th Volkswagen reached the USA in 1960, and in 1963 more Beetles were sold in the USA than in Germany. By 1968 Volkswagen sales in the country had risen to their peak of 423,000

Meanwhile, the cars themselves had been

undergoing steady improvements. Each year brought some technical changes, but the familiar Beetle shape never really seemed to change. You really do need to be a Beetle enthusiast to tell the year of a car at a glance.

The split rear window disappeared in 1953, to be replaced by a small oval-shaped window, and this in turn was replaced by a square rear window in 1957. In 1954, the engine gained an extra 5 bhp, with an increase in capacity to 1192cc to produce 30 bhp and a top speed of 68 mph.

In 1960, the semaphore indicator arms disappeared, to be replaced with modern flashing indicator lamps, and an increased compression ratio and new carburetor saw the engine's power output increased to 34 bhp, in conjunction with a new fully-synchronized transmission. A touch of true luxury came in 1961 with the addition of a fuel gauge!

The rear window was enlarged slightly in 1964, while in 1965, a new Volkswagen 1300 model was introduced, using a 1285cc engine producing 40 bhp. In the following year, a Volkswagen 1500 was launched, with a 1493cc engine pushing the Beetle to a top speed of 125 kph (78 mph) and front disk brakes as standard. An equalizing spring was fitted in this year to all Beetles, in order to prevent the rather sudden handling of the swing-axle rear suspension. In 1967, new square-section bumpers were fitted, along with vertical headlamps, larger rear lights, and a split-circuit braking system. The 1500 model was optionally available with a semi-automatic transmission and a more sophisticated, double-jointed rear suspension. This year also saw the electrical system upgraded to 12 volts from the previous six-volt set-up.

LEFT: Rarest-of-the-rare, a 1939 Beetle in a convoy of pre-'53 cars. Just try getting hold of those scarce grooved bumpers today!

RIGHT: "Peaches 'n' Scream" was built purely to win shows, at a cost of around $20,000. The car features a 2084cc motor with all he hi-po mods you could dream of.

BELOW: A no-frills Standard model Beetle is flanked by two examples of the more luxurious Export model.

Two convertible models had initally been available, produced by the old-established coach-building firms of Hebmüller and Karmann. The Hebmüller car, a two-seater version with a distinctive long rear deck, was produced between 1948 and 1949, although only some 695 cars were constructed before a fire bankrupted the company. The Hebmüller convertibles are, of course, very rare, with only around 50 in existence worldwide in various stages of restoration. The four-seater convertible was manufactured by Karmann, and was produced until 1979, when it was replaced by the Golf Cabriolet.

Volkswagen produced its own coachbuilt car on the Beetle chassis with the introduction of the Volkswagen Karmann Ghia coupé in 1955 and the convertible in 1957. The car was styled by the Italian styling house, Ghia and was hand-built on the Beetle chassis in the Karmann factory in Osnabrück.

In 1969, the USA-market Beetles were fitted with the 1584cc, 47 bhp engine from the Transporter vans. In 1970 the first major change from Porsche's original design was made when the new 1302 model was launched alongside the standard Beetle range. The new model used Mac-Pherson strut front suspension instead of the previous torsion bar design; these cars can be identified by a somewhat more bulbous front end. At the rear of the 1302, double-jointed axles were used, previously only available with the semi-automatic transmission. The new model was available with either 1200, 1300 or 1600 engines. Changes to the 1300 engine, including twin exhaust and inlet ports with a higher compression ratio and improved oil cooling raised its

LEFT: 1957 saw the rear window increased in size to a square shape. Note the period exterior sun visor.

RIGHT & BELOW: This '57 is a prime example of the 'Resto Cal' style. Look closely and check out the angle of those rear wheels after a serious lowering job. The interior is virtually stock.

output to 44 bhp, while similar changes to the 1600 engine boosted it to 50 bhp. The shape of the engine lid was changed to accommodate the greater height of the new engines. The rear window was increased in size again, and a new safety steering wheel was fitted.

A major production milestone was reached in 1972: on February 17, with production of the 15,007,034th car, the Beetle surpassed the production record previously held by the Ford Model T. To commemorate the occasion, a special-edition model was produced, called the "World Champion" or "Weltmeister" Beetle. Based on the 1300 model, these cars had special light blue metallic paint, ten-spoke Lemmerz sports wheels, and a rubber bumper strip.

It was in this year that a further new model was added to the range – the 1303 Beetle. An even more radical departure from Porsche's concept than the 1302, these cars featured a similar mechanical specification to the 1302, but received a new sharply-curved windshield, a shorter hood, and the roof and scuttle were moved further forward; inside, the car used a new full-width sculpted dashboard.

The 1974 model year saw the last Beetle leave the Wolfsburg assembly line, to make way for production of the new Golf model. However, European Beetle production continued in the Hanover, Emden and Brussels factories, with the 18 millionth car leaving the Emden factory in October.

LEFT: Whatever you might think about the style, this matching Swiss Beetle and trailer is a nice piece of workmanship.

RIGHT: This two-seater convertible is based on the UK-manufactured Wizard kit.

BELOW: The Beetle-based sand rail in action – constructed using a Beetle engine in a lightweight tubular chassis.

Meanwhile in the UK, 1974 saw the import of the 250,000th car since 1953, and to commemorate the occasion, some 2500 of the European 1300S model (not available before in the UK) were imported and rebadged as a limited-edition GT Beetle. These cars were based on the standard torsion-bar suspension, flat-screen Beetle, using the 1600 engine, with front disk brakes, special wheels, interior accessories, and available in only three colors: Lemon Yellow, Apple Green and Tomato Red.

Unfortunately, 1975 was to mark the beginning of the end for the Beetle: partly as a result of the unbounded success of the new Golf models, the Beetle range was pruned severely, leaving just the flat-screen, torsion-bar models, although the 1303 body style was continued for the Cabriolet. Beetles were only offered with either a 1200 or 1600 engine, and production of this range carried on until 1978, when the last German-built cars left the factory, and European production ceased.

Beetles were, of course, still being produced in the Mexican and Brazilian factories, and the car was still available in Europe, as Mexican-built cars were imported to Germany. These left-hand drive cars were not, however, sold by Volkswagen in the UK, although many enthusiasts successfully imported Mexican Beetles themselves.

The Mexican-built Beetles differed from their German counterparts in several respects. The cars had the smaller rear windows, as used on German-produced cars between 1965 and 1971, and instead of the alternator fitted to the later European cars, they continued to use a DC generator. Available only with the 1200 engine, Mexican cars featured side trim, fuel gauge, heated rear window, anti-dazzle mirror, passenger grab handle, inertia-reel seatbelts and adjustable headrests. The running boards and the tailpipes were once again chrome-plated.

The Beetle passed another major landmark on May 15, 1981, when the 20 millionth example was produced, marked with a special edition "Silver Bug", featuring silver metallic paintwork and special "20 Millionen" side decals and badging on the engine lid, key fob and gearshift

In 1985, the Beetle celebrated its 50th birthday, and the "Jubilee Beetle" or "JubiläumsKäfer" was produced to mark the event. This was finished in pewter gray metallic paint with tinted green windows, and used the larger rear window as seen on post-'72 European cars together with the bulged rear apron as on post-'75 European cars, while the interior included GTi-style seats, upholstery and steering wheel. Externally, the "JubiläumsKäfer" was distinguished by sports wheels and special "50 Jahre" badging. This model also marked the end of exports to Germany – the Beetle was finally officially unavailable in Europe.

Now that it no longer had to cater for the requirements of export markets, the Mexican factory was able to make several modifications to the Beetle design after 1985, mostly to minimize production costs and optimize the car for local conditions, although some of the Mexican modifications are definitely upgrades. In 1985, the rear heating outlets were discontinued, the engine

LEFT: Brian Burrows' record-breaking *Outrage II* funny car staging a burnout to warm the tires for maximum traction on the start line.

BELOW LEFT: The grunge bug. There's a message in there somewhere.

RIGHT: Terry's Beetle Services' *Moody* in dragstrip action.

BELOW: This classically-styled beach buggy was constructed using a 1955 chassis.

LEFT: Ulf Kaijser's Jungle Green '56 sports around 50 original 1950s accessories, including fender skirts, opening rear windows and all the chrome bits you could ever need.

BELOW LEFT: Antique Beetles gather under the German rain. Second on the right is a rare open four-door Papler police car.

RIGHT: It's hard to believe these two started life in the same factory.

BELOW: Where else but California? A convoy of Beetles and Beetle-based machinery heads for one of the summer's enthusiast gatherings.

and luggage compartment seals were mounted on the lids rather than on the body, halogen headlamps were introduced and the rear noise-deadening material was dropped, along with the heated rear window. For 1986, an intermittent wash/wipe was available and in 1988, the fresh air ventilation system was deleted, and small plastic center caps replaced the metal hubcaps. Electronic ignition was fitted in 1988 and an alarm became standard in 1990. For the 1991 model year, the engine was fitted with a two-way exhaust catalyst with the rear apron being modified to suit the new single tail-pipe. At the same time, the chrome trim for front and rear windows was discontinued and a new style of dashboard was introduced, with a lower radio mounting position and Golf-style switches. A special

taxi model, with no passenger seat fitted, was also introduced.

Production at the Volkswagen do Brasil factory, established in São Paulo in 1953 and producing Beetles since January 1959, ceased in 1986. Despite repeated rumors that production was also to cease at the Mexican factory, which had been producing cars since 1967, the car gained a new lease of life in 1991 when the Mexican government announced a road tax exemption for cars sold below a certain price. The Beetle was the only car to sell below this threshold, and sales increased from 33,000 in 1989 to 86,000 in 1991. Production has continued at about 450 cars a day ever since, and on June 23, 1992, amid a surprising lack of European publicity, Beetle No. 21,000,000 left the Puebla pro-

duction line, again celebrated by a special edition of some 6000, in this case with "21 Millones" badging. The 1992 model Beetles were fitted with a new padded steering wheel, dual-circuit brakes with a tell-tale, inertia reel front seatbelts, and static rear seatbelts. A new GL model was introduced for this year, using a sports steering wheel, chrome hubcaps, passenger door mirror, rear parcel shelf, new front trunk lining and radio speakers in the doors.

Prompted mainly by emissions requirements, changes for the 1993 model year included the adoption of Digifant fuel injection, regulated catalytic converter, hydraulic tappets, dual valve springs and at long last, a proper oil filter. In 1993, it was announced that the Beetle was to begin production again in Brazil. The 1994 Brazilian Beetle was available in two models, to use either gasoline or alcohol-based fuel (widely available in Brazil) and was powered by a 1600cc engine using twin Solex carburetors and producing 58.7 bhp, with electronic ignition and a catalytic converter. New safety equipment included reinforced seat frames, better-quality door locks, laminated windshield glass and front disk brakes.

A trickle of "gray imports" continues to find illegal routes over the border into the USA, and it has even been whispered that the car may be re-introduced to Europe in small numbers as an alternative to the astronomical development costs of a modern small car, and reflecting the growing desire for more individualistic transport in a world of automotive conformity.

One of the major reasons behind the enduring popularity of the Beetle is the great simplicity of the design. Intended from the very beginning to be a "People's Car", the VW was designed around a low price and, in the days where a car was a luxury beyond the reach of an ordinary family, Porsche also designed it to be particularly robust and easily-maintained.

The Beetle is built on a simple floorpan chassis – a tubular backbone runs the length of the car and outriggers carry the floorpans on which the seats are mounted. The backbone is forked at the rear to carry the transmission and the light-weight magnesium alloy engine. Up front, a simple torsion bar suspension design is used, while at the rear end, suspension duties are handled by swing-axles and torsion bars. The bodyshell is bolted directly on to the chassis and can be removed in a matter of hours simply by removing the necessary bolts. On the outside of the body, all four fenders are simply bolted on, making for quick and easy repair.

ABOVE: The Kübelwagen or "Bucket Car" used only rear-wheel drive, but was fitted with a limited-slip differential to give it incredibly good cross-country performance.

ABOVE RIGHT: A 1942 Kübelwagen

RIGHT: No, not another Kübelwagen, but a Volkswagen Type 181, marketed in the USA as the VW 'Thing'. Like the Kübelwagen though, it was based on the Beetle chassis and was developed from military requirements.

OVERLEAF: Look again and you'll see that what Scotty's Baja has gained in height, it's lost in length.

Kits and Customs

With some 21 million Beetles having been sold around the world, there's no shortage of owners wanting to stamp their own personality on their car – the desire to customize Beetles has been around almost as long as the car itself. Right from the earliest days of the Beetle, owners sought to make their cars stand out from the crowd – not a bad idea when you realize just how spartan the interiors of the early cars were.

One of the first to see the potential for upgrading the Beetle's rather basic specification was a former Volkswagen employee, Karl Meier. Having been one of the firm's earliest employees, he was involved after the war in constructing serviceable vehicles by building crude bodywork on to Volkswagen chassis. Most of his creations were simple utility vehicles built during the late 1940s, but a unique Beetle coupé was constructed for an adventurous customer. Perhaps the first radically-customized Beetle, this car was constructed by cutting a Beetle bodyshell in half along its entire length and widening it by over four inches in order to make a coupé.

When Volkswagen ceased supplying chassis to outside body builders in 1949, Karl Meier moved into reupholstering Volkswagen seats in somewhat more attractive fabrics than the austere patterns offered as standard. In time, he produced other accessories and built the business up into the Kamei firm which is well known today, especially in Europe, for its aftermarket customizing and accessory products. The Kamei name will be familiar to a great many Beetle owners as one of the firm's most popular pro-

BELOW LEFT: A Porsche turbo-style "whale tail" is a popular addition.

RIGHT AND FAR RIGHT: Wood-paneled dash and vintage-style gauges are one way to stamp your mark on the Beetle's functional interior . . . on the other hand, dragstrip action may mean a roll cage takes priority.

BELOW: California-based Burton Burton, millionaire and avid Volkswagen collector, poses with a selection of his fleet.

ducts was a plastic cowling – still seen on many Beetles running around today – which fitted over the vents on the rear lid and prevented rain from entering the engine compartment while still allowing the flow of cooling air. Running a close second in the popularity stakes must be the plastic mesh parcel shelf, installed under the dashboard of millions of Beetles and several varieties of this latter item were available from different manufacturers.

Early Beetle accessories included such indispensable devices as cushions for the neck, knees and arms, holders for hats and an extended control for the fuel reserve tap – in the days before Volkswagen added the fuel gauge in 1961, the driver had to simply wait until the car began to run dry and then grovel about under the dashboard to turn to the reserve supply. Many items were later taken up by Volkswagen in production cars, such as a cover for the rear luggage compartment, heel boards below the rear seat, and a proper accelerator pedal where the early cars simply had a small roller.

Of course, Kamei was not the only firm to produce accessories for the Beetle and just about every conceivable extra has been offered for the car, some of them more sensible than others. Flower vases mounted on the dashboard were very popular during the 1950s and 1960s, ashtrays were available to fit the gearlever, "Airolater" flaps could be added to better direct the flow of demisting air on to the windshield and several different designs of rear window heater were produced, along with numerous other decorative items for the interior.

More accessories and developments come on to the market every year to update the Beetle for

ABOVE: "Thinbug" is some 18 in. narrower than a stock Beetle.

LEFT AND ABOVE RIGHT: This is one hot Beetle with a difference. The rear-mounted flat-four has been junked in favor of a 327 cu.in. Chevy V8. The car rides on narrowed Chevy Corsair front suspension, with a Ford rear end and a tube chassis.

RIGHT: From one extreme to the other – the dash-mounted flower vase was a popular 1950s addition.

the 1990s. In just the last few years, we have seen electric heating kits, a strong plastic parcel shelf with a mounting for a modern radio so that the smaller dashboard hole does not need to be enlarged, central consoles, electric window kits, specially-designed speaker mounting pods – the list is endless.

These days, however, largely driven by the popularity of drag-racing, the Beetle scene has moved on from plastic spoilers and extending cigar holders to the more serious business of improving the power of the humble flat-four engine.

The success of the Beetle on the drag strip in the 1960s was mirrored by the growing interest in high-performance Beetles for road use, and pretty soon large numbers of Beetles were seen sporting wide wheels and lurid color schemes, once it became general knowledge that the Beetle really could be made to go fast and handle well.

The Beetle's flat-four air-cooled engine was, of course, originally intended simply to be reliable and cheap to produce and maintain. High performance was probably the last thing on the

PREVIOUS PAGES: The "Thinbug" poses next to a more conventional cousin.

LEFT AND BELOW: This Bug's not only riding low, it's received a pretty radical roof chop as well.

RIGHT: Dual carbs hint at some serious power from this heavily-chromed motor.

BELOW RIGHT: The conventional exterior hides a seriously powerful V8 engine.

minds of those Porsche engineers in the 1930s and the engine was designed deliberately to be under-stressed, being very low-revving and producing a relatively low power output for its size. It was the under-stressed nature of the design which enabled the car to cruise all day at its maximum speed without the engine expiring. It is also the reason why Beetles often achieve such high mileages – in normal use, most enthusiasts will feel cheated if they don't manage to squeeze at least 100,000 miles from an engine and the strength of the basic design means that there's plenty of scope for power upgrades without expensive machining and reinforcing work.

The under-stressed, "unburstable" nature of Porsche's engine was a great thing for the average postwar driver who was more interested in actually arriving at his destination than in peak power outputs and torque curves, but it does mean that the modern-day Beetle tuner has a great deal to play with when it comes to liberating more horsepower from the humble flat-four.

For a car which at first sight would appear to be desperately badly suited to hotting up and to motorsport in general, the Beetle engine has endured an inordinate amount of attention from engineers desperate to extract every last bit of horsepower from the engine. The reason for this is that it is relatively simple to achieve major power gains without a serious stripdown of the

engine. The first tuning work in the 1950s tended to be based around twin carburetor kits to offset the disadvantage of the single central carburetor with its long inlet tract. The early tuning kits also usually offered an oil cooler to combat the common problem of overheating.

In the 1950s, the German-manufactured Oettinger Okrasa TS-1200 kit consisted of a pair of 32 mm Solex carburetors and a pair of dual-port cylinder heads. Also available was a Fram oil filter, to augment the standard Volkswagen filtration system (which consisted of a simple screen behind the drain plate in the sump) and a new oil cooler, a simple copper tube, designed to be mounted in the flow of cooling air – not a terribly effective solution.

The Okrasa TSV-1300 kit was the same, but also included a longer-throw crankshaft to take the 1200 engine up to 1295cc – that's 10cc larger than the later factory 1300 engine. Along with the crankshaft, the kit also provided spacers to extend the pushrods and to fit under the cylinder barrels. Of course, fitting all this gear involved far more work than a simple bolt-on carburetor kit.

The Okrasa kit was never what you could call cheap, but having fitted it all to your Beetle, you could expect some pretty startling performance gains. The TSV-1300 kit took the power output from 30 bhp up to a dizzy 48 bhp at 4200 rpm – enough to take the car to a top speed of over 80 mph, whereas the standard 1200 never managed to struggle much over 70 mph.

Since those early days of Beetle tuning, increasing the engine's capacity has become a common way to pump up the power output. The fact that the cylinders are separate from the crankcase and can be removed from the engine and replaced with big-bore barrel and piston sets means that the capacity of the engine can be increased quite dramatically before expensive engine stripdowns and machining work are required. Beetle tuning has grown massively since the 1960s and it is now possible to build a complete Beetle-style engine without using a single Volkswagen component – even complete heavy-duty crankcases are now being produced, specially designed to cope with the stresses of top-flight drag-racing competition.

ABOVE: The US-style license plate conceals the fact that the Cal looker was built in the UK.

ABOVE RIGHT: Mark Salisbury's back-to-basics roadster uses a completely removable "Carson top" instead of a folding hood.

RIGHT: Ferrari-Testarossa-style side strakes are an owner addition to this Wizard Roadster kit.

Not only the engines have been breathed upon by the tuning experts. There's hardly a single mechanical component on the Beetle which can't be uprated in some way, from simple quick-shift kits to reduce the travel of the gearshift, to complex specially-built five-speed racing transmissions and limited-slip differentials. Much attention has been paid to improving the handling of the cars equipped with swing-axle rear suspension, where the sudden change in camber of the rear wheels can make the handling rather unstable, especially when braking or lifting off in the middle of a bend.

It is generally accepted that one of the single greatest improvements to the car's handling is achieved by lowering the suspension. The simplicity of the Beetle's suspension makes this fairly easy, merely involving welding adjusters into the front axle beam and rotating the rear trailing arms on their splines, and is a popular customizing trick. Disk brake conversions are widely available for the front axle and it's even possible to convert the rear brakes to disks for the diehard go-faster addict. The 1500 model was supplied by the factory equipped with disk brakes on the front axle, and the handling of the later 1302 and 1303 cars, with their double-jointed rear axles and MacPherson strut front suspension, was generally agreed to be better than that of the swing-axle and torsion bar cars. The double-jointed rear axles had previously only been available in conjunction with the semi-automatic transmission.

The home of Beetle customizing is not the car's homeland, but Southern California. For most of the car's lifespan the USA was Volkswagen's major market, overtaking even Germany in the Beetle sales stakes. Drag racing was initially very popular in California, and it was here that Beetles were first modified in large numbers.

Customizing trends come and go as fashions, but one style which has stuck is the "California look", or Cal look. The name arose simply because all those Californians who personalized their cars to make them stand out from the crowd, tended to go for the same modifications. So many cars were adopting the same style that the Cal look was even "officially" recognized in 1975, by California-based *Hot VWs* magazine.

To get that cool Cal look, you'll need to lower your Beetle at both front and rear, giving it a slightly nose-down stance, remove all the exterior chromework and embellishment, squirt a subtle paint color over the bodywork and throw in a high-performance engine. The finishing touch is a classy set of wheels – originally you'd have been able to choose from only a few select styles such as the Speedwell-BRM magnesium alloy design or the EMPI items, but these are pretty rare now. There's a wide range to choose from though, reproductions of the classic EMPI five-spoke and eight-spoke designs being some of the most popular.

The Cal look is just one type of customizing and Beetles have been modified in almost every way you could imagine. Custom tricks range from simply whipping off the bumpers and throwing on a set of chrome running boards, to lowering the roof a few inches and creating forwards-opening "suicide" doors. Engine transplants are pretty common too, whether it's a water-cooled Golf engine, a Porsche unit or even a V8 – it's all been tried somewhere.

Whatever you may think of customized Beetles, the Cal look Beetle seems set to stick around for as long as people can find sound cars to practice their customizing skills on, but another style which follows a close second in terms of popularity is the Baja Bug.

The Baja Bug takes its name from the Baja 1000 race held in the Mexican Baja Desert. The Beetle

RIGHT: A desert racing Karmann Ghia? Not quite – it may look like Volkswagen's hand-built coupé, but underneath the plastic bodywork there's a tubular sand rail chassis.

BELOW: A bolt-on snub nose gives this bug an unlikely air of gravitas.

captured the attention of desert racers who admired it for its ruggedness and the simplicity with which it could be repaired. The suspension design made it simple to raise the car's ground clearance, while the virtually flat underside of the floorpan enabled the car to slide over obstacles which would impede the progress of conventional vehicles. What's more, in the punishing desert heat, the air-cooled engine wouldn't boil and there were no radiator hoses to worry about.

Some racers decided that much of the external bodywork was superfluous and so removed large chunks of the Beetle's front and rear bodywork in order to improve its ground clearance when climbing at steep angles. It was only a short step from that to the addition of fiberglass sections to round off the sharp edges and the Baja Bug became a common sight on both sides of the Atlantic.

Many of the Baja Bugs you'll see on the road today will never see a muddy field let alone a desert race, but a vast range of parts is available to make your Beetle look just like a real Mexican desert racer, from roof-mounted oil coolers to monster wide wheels.

The ease with which the Beetle can be dismantled is one of the main reasons behind its massive popularity as a basis for kit cars and custom projects. When your Beetle has finally had enough of highway life and when the bodywork has been ravaged by rust and accident damage, simply drive it into the garage, unbolt the bodyshell and take it to the nearest wrecking yard. Then go out and buy a shiny new fiberglass bodyshell in whatever style you fancy, whether

it's a buggy, a delivery van or a sports car. Take it home and break out the spanners. A few hours later, you could have a different car.

But special bodies are nothing new, either. As early as 1950, independent coachbuilders were producing their own body designs for the Beetle chassis, often with uprated engines to match the stylish looks. One of the first of these was the

PREVIOUS PAGES: Monster tires mean nothing stops this Baja Bug.

ABOVE: Desert racing isn't limited to Baja Bugs – a standard-looking Beetle will be fine for the job with a few suitable mods.

LEFT: With this much work having gone into dressing up the engine, you can bet that this is one Baja which won't see too much desert action.

RIGHT: A body-lift kit gives this mean machine the perfect Baja pose.

"Denzel 1300", produced by Wolfgang Denzel, who by the mid-1950s was offering 65 bhp from a 1281cc engine using twin 40 mm carburetors, which pushed the car's top speed to around 100 mph.

The Enzmann 506, produced in Switzerland, used an Okrasa TSV-1300 engine conversion in a two-seater bodyshell, to give the lightweight car a top speed of over 100 mph and acceleration from 0-60 mph in just 12 seconds. The hideous Colani GT designed by industrial designer Luigi Colani, was one of the less attractive body styles to grace the VW chassis, and was sold through a mail-order house.

Between 1950 and 1956, the Rometsch-Karosserie company of Berlin produced its hand-built "Beeskow" model, constructed using an aluminum body on a steel and wood frame. The car featured front-opening "suicide" doors, and a single rear seat which was installed sideways in order to increase rear leg-room, with a small luggage area behind it. The Beeskow was succeeded by the "Sport-Kabriolett" model, also available as a coupé, in 1957. This all-new model featured a

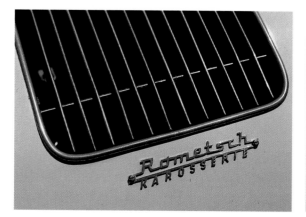

FAR LEFT: The badge of exclusivity: the rare Rometsch Beeskow was hand-built on a Beetle chassis.

ABOVE: A no-frills beach buggy is fitted with special paddle tyres for maximum traction in the sand.

LEFT: A bolt-on enthusiasts dream machine.

RIGHT: The long whip antenna helps buggy drivers to avoid each other in the sand dunes.

different body and used the Okrasa engine conversion.

The Drews "Sport Cabrio" was coachbuilt in aluminum and is now one of the rarest of the coachbuilt cars, while Dannenhauer & Strauss of Stuttgart produced a model which was similar in appearance to the Porsche models of the time. Beutler offered a 2+2 coupé and a Beetle-based station wagon or delivery van. Using as much standard bodywork as possible, the estate and van provided a very small load area and cost half as much again as the Beetle saloon, although the firm did beat VW in the station wagon game by several years.

Hebmüller and Papler also produced four-door open Beetles between 1947 and 1948, for police use. The roof was removed along with all the windows, and most of these cars simply had curtained openings instead of proper doors, although a handful were constructed using proper steel doors.

More recently, the introduction of fiberglass has meant that a massive range of different body styles is available for mounting on the Beetle chassis and it is a relatively simple job for the enthusiast to build a simple beach buggy or a detailed Porsche replica in his own garage.

LEFT: Interior of the four-door police-spec Papler Beetle. Note how the car has canvas strips in place of proper doors.

BELOW LEFT: The Kübelwagen may have been a favorite in World War II, but Baja Beetles never saw military service.

RIGHT: The five-stud wheel fixings mean this buggy's based on a pre-'65 chassis.

BELOW: This stretched limo-style Beetle uses reversed stock Beetle doors at the rear. Four-door Beetle taxis were produced in Berlin for a time during the '50s, but none were quite as outrageous as this creation.

One of the most popular conversions is to turn your worn-out Beetle into a beach buggy – another idea which was born in California. At first, owners looking for low-budget thrills in the sand would simply remove the bodywork and race around on the chassis, with crude bracing added for support – until, that is, someone had the idea of constructing a simple tub-like body from fiberglass and mounting it on the Beetle chassis. Perhaps the first widely-available buggy design was the Manx, produced by Californian Bruce Meyers in 1964, and the first British buggy appeared in 1967 as the "Volksrod".

Die-hard sand racers went one stage further, with the construction of "sand rails". These are purpose-built with a simple tubular chassis frame and the Beetle engine is ideal for this application, as it's a lightweight and compact unit and comes complete with a convenient transaxle. What's more, its self-contained air-cooling system means that cooling radiators and the associated plumbing do not have to be installed. These days though, you'll find sand rails running engines from virtually any source, often with purpose-built suspension.

Of course, the very earliest Porsche sports cars

LEFT AND RIGHT: Radical body mods include a drastic roof chop and front-opening "suicide" doors. More bizarrely, the whole front end hinges up to reveal V8 power.

BELOW: The Beetle chassis in yet another incarnation.

were built using, for the most part, Beetle components and so the Beetle chassis makes an ideal starting point for a pretty accurate replica of the early Porsche models such as the 356 or 550. Indeed, some of these replicas are so close to the real thing that even for the expert, the only way to tell for certain whether or not the car is a fake is to tap the bodywork to find out whether it's made from fiberglass or metal.

The craze for replacing the Beetle bodyshell had even come full-circle by the 1990s. The UK-based firm Wizard Roadsters, which started life supplying roadster-style conversion kits, has developed a full replacement standard bodyshell – in fiberglass. As you might expect, there are a few differences here and there which the eagle-eyed Beetle enthusiast will happily point out, but for the most part it's a replacement bodyshell which just cannot rust. What better way to give your Beetle a new lease of life?

OPPOSITE PAGE: This Wizard Roadster cabriolet conversion also features a Porsche turbo-style bodykit, although this "whale tail" is strictly cosmetic.

RIGHT: This ill-fated and plug-ugly bodykit was a laughing stock during its one and only public appearance, prompting enthusiasts to deluge the vendor in tirades of abuse. It was intended to be a low-cost alternative to standard body styling parts then available.

BELOW: The 1303 models, identified by their bulbous front end and windscreen, are relatively unusual subjects for customizing.

Bug Racing

Back in the 1960s, when a few enthusiasts first tried their luck down the quarter-mile running against the finest Detroit iron, the Beetle was regarded as a joke on the drag-racing scene; a 34 bhp family car was hardly a machine to terrify V8 racers.

However, tuning parts could already be obtained in the USA, thanks to the import of the German Okrasa kits, and together with a few USA-manufactured bits and pieces, the Beetle engine could be turned into a pretty powerful unit. Because of the class structures of the sport, the Beetles suddenly started winning, helped by their light weight and the traction benefits of their rear engine.

At the forefront of Beetle drag racing in those early days was the EMPI firm which came from Riverside, Southern California in the mid-1950s when Joe Vittone established his "Econo Motors" Volkswagen dealership. Noticing the short life of valve components in the air-cooled engines, he began manufacturing replacement valve guides and then branched out into handling components. One of the company's earlier products and one of the most popular, was the so-called camber compensator, which acted as an equalizing spring on the rear suspension to stop the rear wheels of swing-axle cars tucking in under hard cornering. The head of research and development, Dean Lowry, was one of the first to campaign a seriously-competitive Beetle on the drag-strip, recording quarter-mile times of around 14 seconds with his "Inch Pincher".

PREVIOUS PAGES: They may look similar but these are two very different drag cars – look closely and you'll see that the white car has received a major roof chop and is running with a lightweight one-piece plastic front end.

ABOVE AND ABOVE RIGHT: John Brewster's *Street Lethal* drag racer turns in some seriously quick quarter-mile times, and as a bonus it's fully street legal, using a full Beetle body and chassis.

LEFT: Never mess with a man packing a parachute on the back of his Karmann.

RIGHT: This purpose-built "rail" dragster still relies on an air-cooled flat-four engine.

LEFT AND BELOW: Brian Burrows' *Outrage II* funny car is powered by a 2.8-litre engine which pumps out around 700 bhp using nitrous oxide injection, but which uses virtually no standard Volkswagen components!

RIGHT: A massive rear wing aids the high-speed stability of this drag racing Beetle.

BOTTOM: Traction bars keep the lightweight front end on the ground.

EMPI then began branching out in all directions with accessories of every kind for the discerning Beetle driver, and by the late 1960s was able to offer a complete package of extras already attached to a brand new car, sold as the EMPI GTV.

The GTV MkIV, available in 1968, was loaded with no less than 47 separate accessory products. These included paint striping, chromed door handle guards, chrome fender guards, chromed door edge guards, chrome fan belt guards and a simulated walnut dash (well, it was the 1960s after all). Not all the changes were cosmetic, though. The GTV package included a set of heavy-duty shock absorbers, a front anti-roll bar and the EMPI rear camber compensator, finished off with a set of 5.5-in chrome wheels. On the inside, that walnut-effect dash housed an impressive array of extra instrumentation, including tachometer, ammeter, oil pressure and temperature gauges, hiding behind a four-spoke sports steering wheel.

The heart of the GTV package, however, and the main reason why it retailed at $2820 in 1968,

was the engine work. Vittone and partner Dean Lowry tore apart the 1500cc Beetle engine and added a twin-barrel Solex carburetor on a special tubular manifold, a sports exhaust system and a distributor with a revised advance curve. A piston and cylinder set to take the capacity up to 1688cc was an optional extra, together with an EMPI sports camshaft and a competiton clutch. With the full works, the engine was pumping out between 75 and 80 bhp and would easily take the car past the 90 mph mark.

Most of the EMPI parts were available in the UK through the firm of Speedwell, which had a few tricks of its own up its sleeve when it came to making Beetles go faster. British buyers who wanted more speed from their Volkswagen could buy a Speedwell GT conversion. The engine modifications consisted of just three items – a pair of 38 mm Stromberg CD carburetors, a big-bore kit taking the capacity of the 1200 engine out to 1350cc and a sports exhaust system. The package also included a special instrument panel with tachometer and oil pressure and temperature gauges. The suspension re-

around 37 seconds and 71 mph respectively for the standard car.

Although the early drag-racing Beetles were really only mildly modified, constant development over the years soon saw drag-racing Beetles reaching speeds of over 110 mph. The drag Beetles of the 1960s tended to be virtually standard apart from the engine, wheels and tires, but the search for greater power and lighter weight means that these days the front-runners on the dragstrips are using purpose-built racing machinery. The standard chassis is often replaced with a purpose-built lightweight tube chassis, and the steel Beetle body replaced in whole or part with fiberglass replica panels. At the ultimate end of the scale are the "Funny cars", where the engine is usually mounted in front of the driver, in a tube chassis, covered with a fiberglass body which only vaguely resembles a Beetle. Such cars often use nitrous oxide injection and turbocharging, and run at speeds of over 180 mph, turning in quarter-mile times as low as seven seconds.

The craze for speed doesn't stop on the dragstrip, either: there's even a land speed record for a Beetle, achieved at Bonneville Salt Flats using a street-legal car which was able to post a record speed of 132 mph – a real achievement when you consider that this car had to run for several miles at high speed, unlike some of the fragile drag-racing engines, which can be run only for a few

LEFT: Uprating the Beetle engine to produce serious power means dealing with the searing heat produced – a massive array of louvers is one way to solve the problem.

BELOW LEFT: The original Porsche Spyder was bred for the track and this Beetle-based replica continues the tradition.

ABOVE: *Bad News*, sporting an unusual spoiler.

RIGHT: With a powerful engine in the tail, it's all too easy to lift the Beetle's lightweight front end on a hard drag-strip launch.

ceived an uprated anti-roll bar, an EMPI camber compensator and a set of magnesium-alloy Speedwell-BRM wheels – first choice for the Cal-looker in the USA but expensive for the British enthusiast at £28 per pair in 1968. On some cars, a brake servo was also added, hidden away under the back seat. All this kit made the car about a third faster than the standard VW 1200, accelerating from 0-60 mph in about 14 seconds and reaching a top speed of about 87 mph against

seconds and are so highly-stressed that they seem to explode after every few passes down the strip.

The desert and drag strip are not the only places where the People's Car has taken on all comers and walked away with the honors at the end of the day. Unlikely though it may seem for a car which was designed as basic, low-cost transportation for the masses, Beetles have taken their fair share of victories on the track – both in standard form and as single-seater racing cars. From the earliest days, Beetles have been seen in rallying, autocross and circuit racing.

The idea of a proper Beetle racing car began in California (where else?), where single-seaters using tubular chassis with plastic bodywork and powered by standard Beetle mechanical components were raced in private competitions. In 1965, representatives from the Porsche firm watched the cars in action during a trip to the USA and soon became the European importer for the cars, introducing a new racing formula called Formula Vee. Using standard Beetle mechanical components, the sport offered a real low-cost entry to circuit racing, and tight control of the mechanical specifications meant that the costs did not escalate as the popularity of the sport soared. Formula Vee offered exciting, closely-matched racing and even produced some world-class drivers, such as Formula One Champion Niki Lauda.

Formula Vee was later developed into Super Vee racing when use of the more sophisticated

ABOVE AND ABOVE RIGHT: A Beetle-based buggy in action on the famous Pike's Peak hillclimb.

LEFT: The mid-engined set-up in this sand rail reverses the engine and gearbox for better weight distribution.

RIGHT: The Chenowth is one of the most popular sand rail chassis.

ABOVE: Check out the width of the front tires on this mid-engined drag racing rail.

LEFT: Drag racers at the top levels use hardly any stock VW components.

RIGHT: Don't try this one at home – there are few places a Beetle-based buggy or sand rail won't take you.

engines from the Volkswagen Type 4 cars was permitted, along with the double-jointed rear suspension set-up. Since the 1970s, both Super Vee and Formula Vee have declined in prominence and Beetle-based single-seater racing has become a rather obscure branch of motorsport, but with an enthusiastic following nonetheless.

It is not only single-seaters which have brought Beetles to the race track, though. Since 1989, German Beetle fans have been able to follow the "Käfer Cup" series, which includes some nine rounds of circuit races, hillclimbs and slaloms.

The idea spread to the UK in 1992, with the in-troduction of the "Beetle Cup", where the specification of the cars is more tightly controlled than the "Käfer Cup" and which provides an even lower-cost entry to motorsport than Formula Vee ever did. As little as £2000 (and a suitable post-'57 swing-axle Beetle) could put you on the racing track.

The kit vital to success in the series includes an engine, roll-cage, fire extinguisher, racing seat and fireproof clothing. The engines are taken out to 1641cc and use a sports camshaft, heavy-duty oil pump and a 40 mm Dellorto carburetor, which sees the power output jump to around 70 bhp and the top speed nudging 100 mph. To

LEFT: "Burnout" action warms the tires for maximum traction.

BELOW: Diehard desert racers think nothing of performing a full engine rebuild in the middle of nowhere.

RIGHT: Most buggies aren't an ideal shape for high-speed drag racing action – this driver has added a home-made spoiler to add some downforce and keep things under control.

give the drivers a sporting chance of keeping it all on the track, the cars ride on a lowered and stiffened suspension.

Beetles have also been a popular choice for those competing in rallying and rallycross events, where the traction advantages of the rear-mounted engine give the car an advantage which more than offsets its relative lack of power.

The Beetle has been superseded in rallycross by the more modern four-wheel-drive supercars, many of them refugees from the outlawed Group B international rallying class, such as the Audi quattro and Ford RS200. However, Beetle racers don't give up easily, and one man still holding his own against the supercars is Peter Harrold, although it has to be said that his Beetle is more than slightly modified. The car uses a Porsche Carrera five-speed transmission, modified to provide four-wheel drive by driving forwards through a BMW propshaft to front wheels mounted on Golf driveshafts and hubs, with a BMW differential. The engine had previously been developed to produce around 300 bhp, but cylinder head overheating problems led to the use of water-cooled heads. Not just any heads were used though; a pair of 16-valve heads from the Subaru Legacy were bolted on to the engine, and the camshafts are driven by a belt drive from a modified VW crankshaft. Jawa cylinder liners from a speedboat are used, encased in Porsche barrels, together with Kugelfischer mechanical fuel injection and a Garrett T4 turbocharger. The full power potential of this amazing 16-valve turbo, 4wd Beetle is said to be around the 500 bhp mark.

Bizarre Beetles

The basic design of the car is surprisingly watertight, and if you're foolish or unlucky enough to drive your Beetle into a lake you'll be pleased to see that the car will float for a good while before finally going under. The interior of the car is remarkably well sealed and one of Volkswagen's advertising boasts was that the car was so well constructed that in order to close the door it was necessary to open a window slightly to relieve the air pressure.

This is great if you happen to end up in the water through accident, but over the years there have been a great many attempts to turn Beetles into fully seaworthy transport. One of the more successful was the *Schwimmwagen*, produced for the German Army during World War II. Lacking doors and with all the holes in the bodywork sealed, the Schwimmwagen's exhaust and engine air intake were above the water level and

a propeller was fixed to the rear of the engine, driven from the crankshaft pulley. The Schwimmwagen had four-wheel drive and was capable of 50mph on land and 6mph in water.

A floating Beetle may be just within the bounds of reality for most people, but a flying Beetle? Well, Walt Disney's "Herbie" may have been capable of most things, but in the real world it was just the Beetle engine which took to the skies. The Volkswagen engine was used in several light airplane designs during the 1960s and 1970s, where its air-cooling made it an ideal choice, although it was extensively modified for the job, including twin ignition systems. Even today, the Volkswagen engine is a popular choice for many homebuilt light aircraft in a few countries, notably Australia. The Volkswagen industrial engine, based upon the Beetle unit and essentially very similar, was also found in many

PREVIOUS PAGES: A VW trike on Daytona Beach.

BELOW: Another variation on the trike theme.

RIGHT: The Schwimmwagen evolved as an amphibious version of the Kübelwagen.

BELOW RIGHT: Beetle-based tricycles are easy enough to build, by bolting motorcycle forks to the front end of a shortened Beetle floorpan.

applications, ranging from hot-air balloons to mobile saws and cement mixers.

Almost every country where the Beetle was ever sold in large quantities will have at least one Beetle owners' club, and probably an entire Beetle-obsessed subculture. In both Europe and North America, each summer will see Beetle enthusiasts congregating to worship the People's Car, not only participating in car shows but in arcane Beetle-related games.

You'll find competitions to pack the largest number of people into a single Beetle, Beetle pushes where teams race against each other pushing their Beetles, and engine destructions, where a Beetle engine is run flat-out and bets are taken on the length of time it will take to self-destruct. A more recent innovation is the engine-build contest, where teams are given a certain

time limit to build a complete Beetle engine from a pile of parts and to run it for a set length of time.

As with any classic car, people will go to seemingly ridiculous lengths to restore old Beetles found rotting in obscure orchards and barns. In Europe, the recent opening up of the former East Germany has seen some very early cars emerging for restoration. While most enthusiasts will be happy to save just one Beetle from the great scrapyard in the sky, there are a few people who take things one stage beyond that.

In Britain, Chris Clarke is one such fanatic. He has now restored so many Beetles that he has had to construct a special shelving sytem in his barn in order to store them all and plenty more Beetles wait outside for their chance of restoration. Chris wants to preserve one example

from each year during the 1950s and 1960s and he's already well on the way – he restores one car every year and is proud to claim that he's done all the work himself. Chris's interest in Beetles was fueled by his involvement in rallying and autocross during the '60s and '70s, but these days he prefers to preserve standard cars. He doesn't confine his attention to Beetles, either – his collection includes a 1954 VW Type 2 panel van and a 1954 pick-up.

Although Chris may have more Volkswagens in his collection than most, he's by no means unique. Characters such as Burton Burton in the USA and the Beetle Wreckers firm in Australia are well-known throughout the world of VW enthusiasts for their massive collections of classic Volkswagens.

Restoring cars as a hobby is not unusual, but one enterprising firm in the UK has taken things into its own hands and can offer brand new Beetles, built to the buyer's specification. How can this be possible when the only factories manufacturing new Beetles are situated in São Paulo and Puebla? The secret lies in Autobarn's special body jig which enables the firm to accurately align and weld the various panels required to produce a brand new bodyshell, constructed according to the procedures used by Volkswagen itself. Match up the new hand-built Beetle bodyshell with a brand new floorpan chassis, slot in the latest fuel-injected catalyzed engine, and away you go. A Beetle built in this way should last well into the next century.

LEFT AND ABOVE: You could collect for a lifetime and still not have all the different types of toy Beetle which have been produced over the years.

RIGHT: There's a gathering of Beetle enthusiasts every weekend of every summer in most countries around the world.

Index

Acknowledgments

Editor: Judith Millidge
Production: Simon Shelmerdine and Katy Sawyer
Design: David Eldred

We are grateful to the following individuals for permission to use the photographs on the pages noted below.
Colin Burnham: 1, 2-3, 5, 8 (both), 9, 10 (both), 11 (both), 12, 13 (both), 14 (both), 15, 16 (both), 17, 18, 19 (both), 20 (both), 21 (below), 22, 25 (below), 26 (below), 28 (both), 29 (below), 30, 31 (both), 32-3, 34, 35 (all 3), 36 (both), 37 (both), 38-9, 40 (both), 41 (both), 45 (top), 46-7, 48 (both), 49, 50 (middle & below), 52 (both), 53 (below), 54 (both), 55, 58-9, 60 (below), 64 (top), 65 (below), 66 (below), 67 (below), 70 (both), 71, 75 (top), 78, 79 (both)
Mike Key: 6-7, 21 (top), 23 (both), 25 (top), 26 (top), 27 (both), 29 (top), 42, 43 (both), 44-5, 56 (both), 57 (below), 60 (top), 61 (both), 62 (both), 63 (both), 64 (below), 65 (top), 68 (both), 76 (top), 77
Andrew Morland: 24, 50 (top), 51, 53, (top), 57 (top), 66 (top), 67 (top), 69, 72-3, 74, 75 (below), 76 (below)